Certified Food Safety Manager Exam (CPFM) Study Guide 2022

Gregrey Michael Carpenter

ISBN: 9781986551137

CONTENTS

CH 1 Introduction

Approximately 48 million Americans contract *foodborne illnesses* each year. Stopping an individual illness is tough. However, if we focus on preventing *foodborne illness outbreaks*, which is when 2 or more people get sick from the same food, then we can stop the spread of some of these diseases.

There are 3 forms of contamination, *biological, chemical and physical.*

Biological contaminants are the tiny living creatures we find in and around our foods.

Chemicals are things like cleaners, sanitizers and polishes.

Physical hazards are the bits of bone, plastic or any other foreign object that is not supposed to be in the food.

The centers for disease control and prevention investigate food born illness outbreaks. You will be asked to understand the 5 most common risk factors responsible for these outbreaks.

1. Food is purchased from an unsafe source
2. The food is not cooked correctly
3. The food is held at incorrect temperatures
4. Using contaminated equipment
5. Practicing poor personal hygiene

When a food born illness outbreak occurs generally it is from one of these 5 factors. We will be focusing on how to prevent these things.

There are 4 ways that the food in your facility can become unsafe.

1. ***Time-Temperature abuse***, this is when food is left out for too long at the wrong temperature.
2. *Cross contamination* is when germs are transferred from one place to another.
3. *Poor personal hygiene* has everything to do with the body.
4. *Poor cleaning and sanitizing* is not knowing how or when to clean things.

Foods are classified into 2 groups, *TCS and Ready To Eat. (RTE)*

TCS foods have certain characteristic that we know allow germs/pathogens to grow on them. Plus, since they have all caused foodborne illness outbreaks in the past then we know to be careful with them.

RAW Eggs, Fish, Shellfish, Poultry, Meat, Soy, Milk, Heat Treated Plants, Baked Potatoes

RTE foods are exactly what they are called, they are ***ready to eat***! They have been ***cooked, washed or prepared***

and are not going to have anything more done to them to make them safe.

High Risk Populations are people that are more likely to get sick from food and make up the largest group of people who die from food borne illness, approximately 3000 per year. This group includes anybody with a weakened immune system such the ***elderly and children***. There are special procedures you will need to know when dealing with these groups. We will highlight these procedures when they apply.

There are many government agencies involved in keeping food safe in the United States.

- The *FDA* writes the ***model food code***. Be careful, because this food code is the minimum standards that you must follow and is only a recommendation. This is what the test is based on so be careful, what your company or even your health inspector asks you to do may different than what the food code says.
- The USDA is responsible for the inspection of ***meat poultry and eggs***.
- Each ***state adopts the model food code*** and makes laws from it. Be careful, the laws you follow are state laws and may not be the same as what you are being tested on.
- The ***local regulatory agencies/health department*** adopt the state laws and send inspectors to your facility to uphold the standards.

Chapter 1 QUICK QUIZ *(answers on page 41)*

1. Which is a ready to eat food? (circle one)

A. Crushed Red Pepper B. Raw Fish C. Raw Steak D. Unwashed Lettuce

2. Ground beef patties are left out at room temperature on a prep table, what risk would cause a food borne illness? (circle one)

A. Poor sanitation B. Cross-contamination C. Time-temperature abuse D. Poor hygiene

3. Which of these is considered a TCS food? (circle one)

A. Uncooked rice B. Baked potato C. Whole watermelon D. Sliced bread

Notes:

____

____

____

____

Notes:

Ch 2 The Forms of Contamination

Contamination comes from a variety of places;

1. The animals we use for food
2. Air, contaminated water and soil
3. People-Deliberately or accidentally

The most common way people contaminate food is when they ***don't wash their hands after using the restroom***. When someone consumes food touched by the food handler that didn't wash their hands a food borne illness may occur. This is also called the ***fecal-oral route*** of contamination.

Microorganisms are tiny creatures that are found almost everywhere in the world. For the most part they are good, we like microorganisms. But, there is a tiny group of these microorganisms that we know can make people sick, these are called ***pathogens*** or you might refer to them as germs.

You should also be aware of the word ***toxin*** which is just another word for poison. This is important because some pathogens make toxins which cannot be killed by cooking.

As most of us are aware, the symptoms of a food borne illness can be terrible. ***Nausea, fever and abdominal pain*** are bad enough but vomiting and diarrhea, no thanks! There is another symptom to be aware of called ***jaundice*** which is a yellowing of the skin and eyes. We often hear of babies being born with ***jaundice*** but for this class you need to know it is a liver problem.

An ***onset time*** is a description of how long it takes after eating a contaminated food to show the symptoms. It can be anywhere from ***30 minutes to 6 weeks***.

There are 4 types of ***biological contaminants*** bacteria, viruses, parasites and fungi.

According to the FDA there are ***6 major types of bacteria, viruses, parasites and molds that they consider to be highly contagious*** and lead to severe illness. These are:

- Shigella spp
- Salmonella Typhi
- Nontyphoidal Salmonella
- E-Coli
- Hepatitis A
- Norovirus

Bacteria

Bacteria are found nearly everywhere and because they are not visible on our food we must treat all food as if it were contaminated to prevent illness.

Bacteria will only grow if there are 6 conditions present. We use an acronym to describe these conditions called

FATTOM

Food - Bacteria need nutrients, specifically they need carbohydrates or protein. You will notice all of the foods on the TCS list have carbohydrates or protein.

Acidity - Bacteria only grow in food with little to no acid. Pay attention to the acidity of food on the TCS list.

Temperature - Bacteria grow well between 41° and 135°. This is known as the temperature danger zone.

Time - It takes at least 4 hours for bacteria to grow to an unsafe level.

Oxygen - Many bacteria need oxygen to grow but there are some bacteria that can grow without it.

Moisture – Bacteria need foods that have high levels of moisture, at least .85 water activity (Aw) or above. All of the foods on the TCS list fit these criteria for water. Remember, retail establishments are only allowed to control two of these 6 conditions, time and temperature which is what we will be focusing on during your training. There are 4 specific bacteria we are going to focus on. The FDA has identified these as highly contagious and can cause severe illness.

Non-Typhoidal Salmonella	**Source:** Farm animals	Shigella	**Source:** Human Feces
	Foods Linked To Outbreaks: Poultry, Eggs, Meat and Produce		**Foods Linked To Outbreaks:** Food commonly touched by hands and Flies
	Prevention: Cooking food, especially chicken, to correct temperatures		**Prevention:** Hand washing and controlling flies inside and outside of the facility
Salmonella Typhi	**Source**: People	Eschericia coli	**Source**: Intestine of cattle
	Foods Linked To Outbreaks: Ready to eat foods and beverages		**Foods Linked To Outbreaks**: Ground beef and produce
	Prevention: Hand washing		**Prevention**: Cooking food to correct temperatures and purchase food for a safe source

Viruses

Viruses don't grow in food the way bacteria do. They require a host to grow which can be human or animal. They are often transferred through food but can remain infectious on any surface for long periods of time. Cooking doesn't kill viruses so the best way to prevent the spread of the disease is through good personal hygiene

Hepatitis A (Jaundice)	**Source**: Human Feces	Norovirus (Food Poisoning)	**Source**: Human Feces
	Foods Linked To Outbreaks: Ready to eat foods and shellfish		**Foods Linked To Outbreaks**: Ready to eat foods and shellfish
	Prevention: Wash hands, don't touch food with bare hands and by shellfish from an approved source		**Prevention**: Wash hands, don't touch food with bare hands and by shellfish from an approved source

Parasites

Parasites are typically found in the wild. Parasites don't usually infect our meat or poultry because the food we use to feed our farm animals is treated for safety before we feed them. Parasites are often found in wild animals such as fish and wild game because it is impossible for us to treat their food.

Cooking and freezing kills parasites and it is important to always buy food from an approved supplier.

Fungi

There are 3 types of fungi; yeast, mold, and mushrooms. Fungi will grow in conditions that other microorganisms won't such as foods with low water activity and high acidity. It is always best to discard food with fungus growing on it. Also, only purchase mushrooms from an approved source.

Chemical Contaminants

Certain types of metals contain chemicals that are poisonous to people. Metals such as copper, pewter, lead and zinc can have a chemical reaction when they are in contact with acid or acidic food. This reaction can leach the toxins from the metal and into the food. This is known as toxic metal poisoning. Physical Contamination Bones from ground beef, metal shavings from a can or glass in ice are foreign objects that don't belong in food. These physical contaminants can cause mild to fatal injuries such as choking, cuts or dental damage. The best way to prevent physical contamination is to inspect your food and purchase it from an approved source.

A.L.E.R.T

ALERT is a tool created for the FDA to prevent the deliberate contamination of food. This could be anyone from terrorist or activist to disgruntled staff or even vendors or competitors. Alert stands for

Assure-Make sure products are received from a safe source
Look– Monitor the security of the products in your facility
Employees- Know who is in your facility
Report-Keep information related to food defense accessible
Threat- Develop a plan for responding to suspicious activity or a threat to your facility

Biological Toxins

Another type of contamination comes from things that naturally occur in the environment such as poisonous plants and algae. If the food youpurchase doesn't come from an approved source they may have gotten it from an unsafe place. Two types that are commonly associated with fish are Scombroid toxin and Ciguatera toxin.

Responding to an outbreak

1. Gather information
2. Notify authorities
3. Segregate product
4. Document information
5. Identify staff
6. Cooperate with authorities
7. Review procedures

Food Allergens

Some people are sensitive to specific proteins that naturally occur in food. This is known as a food allergy. Peoples sensitivities vary in severity. Some people experience minor symptoms like hives, rashes and swelling of body parts. Some symptoms might be more severe such as the symptoms that occurs with food borne illness. While others experience reactions that could shut their body down and may cause death, this is known asanaphylaxis.

These are the most common food allergens.

Milk	*Tree Nuts*
Eggs	*Fish*
Soy	*Crustaceans*
Peanuts	*Wheat*

To prevent an allergic reaction, you and your staff must know the ingredients that are in your food. Its best to suggest simple food items and hand deliver food to guests with food allergies.

Cross Contact is the term we use to describe when the food that someone is allergic to touches or gets mixed with the food item they are eating. This could happen through cooking equipment, gloves or even through fryer oil.

Chapter 2 QUICK QUIZ *(answers on page 41)*

1. What is the most important way to prevent foodborne illness from a virus? (circle one) A. Practice good personal hygiene B. Control time-temperature C. Sanitizing D. Preventing cross contamination

2. What foods are Parasites usually connected to? (circle one)
A. Seafood B. Canned Food C. Potatoes D. Cut melons

3. How should a food handler prevent allergens from being transferred onto food? (circle one)
A. Cook food to the correct internal temperature B. Hold hot food at 135 degrees or higher
C. Store food in correctly labelled containers D. Proper handwashing

Notes:

____

____

____

____

____

____

Notes:

Ch 3 The Safe Food Handler

Pay attention to your employee's behaviors, they might not be paying as much attention as you might think. Watch for things like ***touching the hair, face or body.*** Pathogens can easily be transferred this way to food.

Operations need a ***personal hygiene program*** in order to prevent contamination and maintain the cleanliness of the business. It is your responsibility as a manager to maintain the program.

The Handwashing Procedure

Handwashing should be done in a designated sinks only and never in sinks designated for food prep, dishwashing or discarding waste water.

The handwashing procedure is a 5 step process that from beginning to end should take a total of 20 seconds. When complete consider a paper towel to touch the door handle and turn off the faucet.

1. Wet hands with warm running water.
2. Apply enough soap to build up a good lather.
3. Scrub hands and arms vigorously for 10-15 seconds. Pay attention to finger nails and between fingers.
4. Rinse hands and arms thoroughly under running water.
5. Dry hands and arms with either a single use paper towel or a warm dryer.

Employees will also need to be taught ***when to wash their hands.*** They are required to wash their hands ***before they handle food and after they are dirty.*** Here are some examples:

1. Using the restroom
2. Handling raw meat, poultry, and seafood (before and after)
3. Touching the hair, face, or body
4. Sneezing, coughing, or using a tissue
5. Eating, drinking, smoking, or chewing gum or tobacco
6. Handling chemicals that might affect food safety
7. Taking out garbage
8. Clearing tables or busing dirty dishes
9. Touching clothing or aprons
10. Handling money
11. Leaving and returning to the kitchen/prep area
12. Handling service animals or aquatic animals
13. Touching anything else that may contaminate hands

Hand sanitizers/antiseptics may never be used in place of handwashing., and they must be FDA approved.

Hand Care

Fingernails must be kept short and clean. No false nails! No nail polish or gels! With one exception, if the food handler wears single use gloves they may have false nails and nail polish.

If Food handlers work with knives and fire, therefore they will get cuts and burns. When a food handler gets a ***cut or a burn*** it must be covered with a bandage and the bandage must be covered with either a glove or finger cot.

Gloves

Gloves are and excellent tool for keeping pathogens from transferring to food by a food handler's hands. Gloves **should** be used when handling **ready to eat food**. However, gloves must be handled correctly or the gloves themselves can become a problem. First of all, hands must be washed before putting on gloves and make sure to look for strange behaviors from your staff when wearing gloves such as:

1. Washing and reusing gloves
2. Blowing into gloves
3. Rolling gloves up to make them easier to put on

Also, gloves must be changed:

1. A soon as they become dirty or torn
2. Before beginning a different task
3. After an interruption i.e phone call
4. After handling raw meat, seafood, or poultry and before handling ready-to-eat food
5. After four hours of continuous use

Remember, do not handle ready to eat food with your bare hands. Never handle ready to eat food with your bare hands when serving primarily high risk populations

Work Attire

Food handlers must:

1. Wear a clean hat or other hair restraint. No false lashes or hair restraints that could become a physical contaminant. Food handlers with facial hair must wear a beard restraint.
2. Wear clean clothing daily
3. Remove aprons when leaving food-preparation areas. Never wipe your hands on your apron.
4. Remove jewelry from hands and arms before prepping food. Food handlers cannot wear
   - Rings (unless it's a plain band)
   - Bracelets (including medical bracelets)
   - Watches

Food handlers must not *eat, drink, smoke, or chew gum or tobacco when*:

1. Prepping or serving food
2. Working in prep areas
3. Working in areas used to clean utensils and equipment

Staff Illnesses

Generally, if an employee is sick they must either be restricted from handling food or food contact surfaces or excluded from the operation. If an employee has the following symptoms:

Symptom	Restrict/ Exclude	Doctors Note	Contact Health Department
Sore throat with fever or symptoms that can be controlled with medicine	Restrict for general public. Exclude if working with high risk population	No Yes	No No
Vomit, Diarrhea or Jaundice	Exclude	Only to return within 24 hours of last symptom	No
Diagnosed with a specific illness such as any of the "Big 5"	Exclude	Yes	Yes - Report

Chapter 3 QUICK QUIZ *(answers on page 41)*

1. How often should a food handler change their gloves (circle one) A. After 30 mins of handling raw beef B. After 4 hours of continuous use C. After his/her shift

D. Before the shift starts

2. An employee calls in sick and says they have diarrhea and nausea, what should you do? (circle one)

A. Tell the employee to come in until someone can cover for them B. Tell them to take a nap and show up later C. Tell them to stay away from work until the symptoms have passed D. Tell them to call the doctor to make an appointment but come to work in the meantime.

3. What is the minimum time you should scrub your hands with soap when handwashing? (circle one)

A. 5 seconds B. 10 seconds C. 20 seconds D. 40 seconds

Notes:

CH 4 The Flow Of Food

The ***flow of food*** is an important concept to understand. It is all of the steps food takes as it moves through your operation. It begins from the time you ***purchase*** food and follows a trail all the way to the time when you ***serve*** it to the customer.

During the flow of food, it is important that we prevent time-temperature abuse and cross contamination.

Preventing Time-Temperature Abuse

- Monitoring – Learn what items need to be checked and when
- Tools – Make sure all types of thermometers are available to staff
- Recording – Check and record food temperatures regularly
- Procedures – Have procedures that limit how long the food stays in the temperature danger zone
- Corrective Action – Ensure staff knows what to do if standards are not met

Preventing Cross Contamination

- Use Correct Equipment – Use separate equipment for raw and ready to eat food
- Clean and Sanitize – Do this before and after tasks
- Timing – Prepare raw and ready to eat food at different times
- Purchasing – Buy foods that need little handling

Food in the range between 41° and 135° for ***longer than 4 hours*** has been time temperature abused and must be thrown away. But you must also know that most ***pathogens grow much faster when they are between 70° and 125°***. This is a common temperature for kitchens.

Using Thermometers

Bimetallic Stemmed Thermometer

This type of thermometer is simple and must calibrated regularly. It can be immersed into 32° ice water and adjusted by holding the calibration nut and twisting the head of the thermometer until it reads 32°.

Thermocouples and Thermistors

a.k.a Digital Thermometer Measure Temperatures through a metal probe and often come with multiple types. An immersion probe is used for liquids while an air probe is for room temperatures.
The penetration probe is the most common and used for dense objects.

Infrared Thermometers

Infrared thermometers give you a quick and easy digital read out without even touching the food. The biggest problem is they only take surface temps so you will still need a probe style thermometer.

Don't forget, thermometers must be cleaned and sanitized before and after you use them. You must also calibrate your thermometer each shift. It is best to always put the thermometer in the thickest part of a product and you may need to take more than one reading in different spots. Finally, don't write down the temperature on you log until the device steadies.

Chapter 4 QUICK QUIZ *(answers on page 41)*

1. Which thermometer should be used to check the internal temperature of a steak? (circle one) A. Penetration probe B. Immersion probe C. Surface probe D. Air probe
2. What practice can help prevent time-temperature abuse? (circle one) A. Making sure employees are washing their hands correctly B. Sanitizing equipment regularly C. Limiting the amount of food removed from a fridge for prepping D. Scheduling employees for no more than 6 hours.
3. Which practice can help prevent cross-contamination? (circle one) A. Purchasing food from the same supplier B. Using color coded cutting boards C. Using the same cutting board to prepare raw chicken and ready to eat food D. Rinsing the cutting board in a sink between prepping foods.

Notes:

CH 5 Purchasing, Receiving and Storing Food

General Purchasing and Receiving Principals

Purchase food from approved, reputable suppliers: Approved sources have been inspected and meet all applicable local, state, and federal laws. This could be from major food distributors or your local grocery store. Arrange deliveries so when they arrive your staff has enough time to do inspections and they can be correctly received. Try to avoid busy operating hours. Make specific staff responsible for receiving and train them to follow food safety guidelines. Store items promptly after receiving.

Key drop deliveries: Supplier is given after-hour access to the operation to make deliveries. Key drop deliveries must meet the following criteria. Be inspected upon arrival at the operation. Be from an approved source and have been placed in the correct storage location to maintain the required temperature

Rejecting deliveries: Separate rejected items from accepted items. Tell the delivery person what is wrong with the item. Get a signed adjustment or credit slip before giving the rejected item to the delivery person. Log the incident on the invoice or receiving document

Recalls: Identify the recalled food items and remove the item from inventory. Place it in a secure and appropriate location. Store the item separately from food, utensils, equipment, linens, and single-use items. Label the item in a way that will prevent it from being placed back in inventory and inform staff not to use the product. Refer to the vendor's notification or recall notice to determine what to do with the item.

Checking the temperature of received foods

- Meat Poultry and Fish – Insert probe into the thickest part of the meat
- ROP (reduced oxygen packaging) Food – Insert the probe between2 packages or fold package around the probe
- Other packaged food – Open the package and insert the probe into the food
- *Temperature criteria for deliveries:*

Cold TCS food: Receive at 41˚F (5˚C) or lower, unless otherwise specified
Live shellfish: Receive oysters, mussels, clams, and scallops at an air temperature of 45˚F (7˚C) and an internal temperature no greater than 50˚F (10˚C)
Once received, the shellfish must be cooled to 41˚F (5˚C) or lower in four hours

Shucked shellfish: Receive at 45˚F (7˚C) or lower
Cool the shellfish to 41˚F (5˚F) or lower in four hours
Shell eggs: Receive at an air temperature of 45°F (7°C) or lower

Milk: Receive at 45°F (7°C) or lower and cool the milk to 41°F (5°C) or lower in four hour
Hot TCS food: Receive at 135°F (57°C) or higher

Frozen foods must be frozen when received. Look for large chunks of ice or any other indication that the food was thawed and refrozen such as water stains. You don't know how long it was thawed for or to what temperature.

All *packaged* foods including cans need to be inspected for the following and rejected if found:

- Severe and deeps dents in seams or body of the can
- Swollen or bulging ends
- Missing labels
- Holes, leaking or dampness
- Rust
- Signs of pests or pest damage. Pests commonly enter facilities through food deliveries.
- Expiration date. Do not accept food that is missing a date or is past the expiration date.

You may see other dates on labels. A sell-by date tells the store how long to display the product for sale. A best-by date is the date by which the product should be eaten for best quality.

Indicators of time and temperature abuse: If any of these things seem off to you, reject the food.

- Color: Reject food that is moldy or has an abnormal color.
- Texture: Meat, fish and poultry should not be slimy, sticky or dry and should not leave an imprint when pressed on.
- Smell: Look for off smells.

Documents

Shellfish and fish that will be eaten raw or partially cooked must be received with the correct documentation.

Shellfish must be received with a shellstock tag. This tag states where and when the shellfish was harvested and that it was purchased from an approved source. Do NOT remove the shellfish tag from the container until the last shellfish is used. When this last shellfish is used, record that date on the shellstock tag and keep on file for 90 days from that date. Fish that will be eaten raw or partially cooked must be received with documents showing the fish was frozen correctly before you received it. If it was farm raised it must have documentation showing it was raised to FDA standards. Keep these documents for 90 days from the sale of the fish.

Storage

Labeling food for use in a kitchen only requires 2 things to be on the label, the name of the food (unless it is completely obvious) and the expiration date.
Labeling for retail sales requires a lot more information.

- Common name of the food or a statement clearly identifying it
- Quantity of the food
- If the item contains two or more ingredients, list the ingredients in descending order by weight
- List of artificial colors and flavors in the food including chemical preservatives
- Name and place of business of the manufacturer, packer, or distributor
- Source of each major food allergen contained in the food

Marking Dates

TCS Food that will be stored for longer than 24 hours must have a label that indicates when the food must be sold, eaten or thrown out. Ready-to-eat TCS food can be stored for only 7 days if it is held at 41°F or lower. The count begins on the day the food was prepared. For example a food handler that prepared tuna salad on August 1st would need to write a discard date of August 7th on the label.
When combining foods with different use-by dates record the discard date based on the earliest use-by date of all items of food used in the dish.

Temperatures

- TCS Food needs to be stored at an internal temperature of 41°F or lower or 135°F or higher.
- Frozen food must be stored at a temperature that will keep it frozen
- Storage units need to have at least one air temperature measuring device and must be accurate to +/- 3°F. This device needs to be placed in the warmest part of the refrigeration unit and the coldest part of the hot holding unit.
- Do not overload cooler or freezers – this will affect the temperature which can affect food safety
- Use open shelving and do not line the shelves with foil, sheet pans or paper
- Monitor temperatures regularly by sampling at random times. If the temperature is incorrect, discard the food.

Food Rotation

One way to rotate products correctly is to follow FIFO (First in First Out)

1. Identify the food item's use-by or expiration date
2. Store items with the earliest use-by or expiration dates in front of items with later dates
3. Once shelved, use those items stored in front first
4. Throw out food that has passed its manufacturer's use-by or expiration date

Storage Order

The below chart shows how food should be stored on shelving from the top to the bottom, in order to limit cross contamination. You can see that the storage level is based on the cooking temperatures of the food with the highest cooking temperature stored at the bottom.

Storage Order (Top to bottom)	Minimum Cooking Temperature
Ready-to-eat food	135°F
Seafood	145°F
Whole cuts of beef and pork	145°F
Ground meat and ground fish	155°F
Whole and ground poultry	165°F

***Chapter 5 QUICK QUIZ** (answers on page 41)*

1. What is the correct temperature to receive cold food? (circle one) A. 32°F or lower B. 41°F or lower C. 45°F or lower D. 50°F or lower

2. When must you discard potato salad that has been prepared on November 19th? (circle one) A. November 21st B. November 23rd C. November 25th D. November 27th

3. How many inches from the floor should floor should food be stored? (circle one) A. At least 2 inches B. At least 1 inch C. At least 4 inches D. At least 6 inches

Notes:

CH 6 Preparation

Preparation Practices

It doesn't matter whether you are preparing filets at a steakhouse or fruit at coffee shop, you should always follow the guidelines below:

- *Equipment* – Keep clean and sanitized (sanitation specs, ch. 10)
- *Quantity* – Only remove enough cold foods from the fridge that you can prep in a short period of time 4hr
- *Storage* – Return the food you have prepped back to the cooler as soon as possible
- *Additives* – IF you use additives make sure they are approved and NEVER use more than allowed by law and NEVER use the additives to change the appearance of food.
- *Presentation* – Food must be presented to the customer in a way not to mislead or misinform them. Use or colored wraps, additives or lighting must not be used for this.
- *Corrective Action* – If food becomes unsafe for any reason it must be discarded.

Preparing Certain Foods

There are some foods that need special care when preparing. Generally, these are foods are TCS foods.

Produce

- *Cross Contamination* – Make sure when preparing produce that they do NOT touch surfaces that have been use to prep raw meat, seafood etc
- *Washing* – All produce must be washed under running water and...
    - The water must be slightly warmer than the produce
    - Pay close attention to leafy greens i.e spinach, lettuce etc
- *Soaking* – If you are going to soak or store your produce don't mix batches or items
- *Freshly Cut Produce* – TCS produce items such as cut tomatoes, chopped leafy greens and cut melons need to be held at 41°F or below.
- *Raw Seed Sprouts* – If you primarily serve a high risk population do NOT serve raw seed sprouts.

Eggs

- *Pooled Eggs* – These are eggs that have been cracked open and combined in a container. These need to be cooked promptly after mixing or stored at 41°F or below.
- *Pasteurized Eggs* – Use these types of eggs if you are making a dish that needs little or no cooking and also if you mainly serve high risk populations.

Salads Containing TCS Food

Time	Days
4 Hr	7

We've all heard the horror stories with people getting sick after they ate the potato salad at the neighbor's BBQ and there's a good reason why. These salads need to be handled with special attention.

- Only use leftover TCS food like pasta, chicken and salad if you know that it was previously handled correctly with clean hands and temperature control

Ice

Consumption – Only make ice with water that is safe to drink (potable) and hasn't been used to keep other food cold.

Containers and Scoops – Store scoops outside the ice machine and NEVER hold or carry ice in containers that have held raw meats or chemicals. NEVER touch the ice with your hands or a glass scoop.

Variances/HACCP

Certain ways of preparing food require a document that allows a regulatory requirement to be waived, this is called a variance. When applying for a variance some agencies require you submit a HACCP plan. The plan shows how you can account for any food safety risks that may occur while prepping the food item. You need a variance if you...

- Package fresh juice on-site for sale at a later time
- Smoke food as a way to preserve it
- Use food additives or vinegar to preserve foods
- Cure food
- Custom process animals for personal use
- Packing foods using the ROP method
- Spout seeds or beans
- Offer live shellfish from a display tank

Frozen Food – Thawing

When you thaw frozen food you expose it to the temperature danger zone. You should NEVER thaw food at room temperature. Below are the recommended ways to thaw food correctly and safely.

Refrigeration Thaw in the cooler but keep the temp below 41°F

Running Water Thaw in a clean sanitized prep sink under running, drinkable ***water at 70°F***

Microwave Only if it will be cooked immediately after thawing

Cooking As part of the cooking process

Cooking Food

The main reason we cook food is to reduce pathogens in food to safe levels. This is done by cooking each food to its correct ***minimum internal temperature***. Each food has a different temperature depending on the level of hazard the food presents. The more hazardous the food is the higher the temperature.

Food	Minimum Internal Cooking Temp	Length of Time at this Temp
Poultry: (including whole or ground chicken, turkey, and duck)	165°F (74°C)	15 seconds
TCS Food in a Microwave Meat, Seafood, Poultry and Eggs	165°F (74°C)	15 seconds
Stuffed Meat and Stuffing (When stuffed with meat, seafood, poultry or pasta)	165°F (74°C)	15 seconds
Dishes that include previously cooked TCS ingredients	165°F (74°C)	15 seconds
Ground or Mechanically Tenderized Meat and Fish (including beef, pork, other meat)	155°F (68°C)	15 seconds
Injected Meat	155°F (68°C)	15 seconds
Shell Eggs that will be hot-held	155°F (68°C)	15 seconds
Pork, Beef, Veal, Lamb	Stk/Chops: 145°F (63°C) Roasts: 145°F (63°C)	15 seconds 4 Minutes
Eggs for immediate service	145°F (63°C)	15 seconds
Fish	145°F (63°C)	15 seconds
Commercially processed, ready-to- eat food that will be hot-held for service (cheese sticks, fried vegetables, chicken wings, etc.)	135°F (57°C)	15 seconds

You must cook food to these required minimum internal cooking temps unless a customer requests otherwise. If your menu includes TCS foods that are raw or undercooked, you must disclose this on your menu. The also FDA advises against offering raw or undercooked TCS foods on a childrens menu. If you MAINLY serve a high risk population i.e nursing home do not serve the following:

- Raw seed sprouts
- Raw meat, seafood or undercooked eggs (pasteurized are not TCS),
- Unpasteurized milk or juice

Microwave Cooking

TCS food cooked in the microwave need to be cooked to 165°F and these guidelines need to be followed:

- Always cover food to prevent drying
- Rotate food halfway
- Let stand after cooking for 2 mins
- Check the temperature in 2 places

Partially Cooking Foods (par cooking)
When partially cooking foods you must follow these steps to ensure food safety:

1. Do not cook food for more than 60 minutes during the initial cooking period.
2. Cool immediately after cooking
3. Freeze or refrigerate after cooling and make sure it is being held at 41°F or below. Store away from ready to eat foods.
4. Cook or reheat the foods to 165° before serving it.

If you par-cook food your regulatory agency may require you have written procedures in places to show you have handled the food correctly.

Cooling

Cool food from ***135°F to 70°F (57°C to 21°C) within two hours***. then from ***70°F to 41°F within 4 hours***. The total cooling time cannot be longer than six hours

Before cooling food, start by reducing its size: Cut larger items into smaller pieces. Divide large containers of food into smaller containers or shallow pans.

Methods for cooling food safely and quickly:

- Place food in an ice-water bath
- Stir it with an ice paddle
- Place it in a blast chiller

Reheating Foods

Food reheated for immediate ***service can be reheated to any temperature if it was cooked and cooled correctly***. Food reheated for hot-***holding must be reheated to an internal temperature of 165°F (74°C) for 15 seconds within two hours***. Reheat commercially processed and packaged ready-to-eat food to an internal temperature of at least 135°F (57°C).

Remember... Food must be thrown out in the following situations:

- When it is handled by staff who have been restricted or excluded from the operation due to illness
- When it is contaminated by hands or bodily fluids from the nose or mouth
- When it has exceeded the time and temperature requirements designed to keep food safe

Chapter 6 QUICK QUIZ *(answers on page 41)*
1. While cooling TCS food, the temperature must go from 135°F to 70°F in how much time? A. 2 hours B. 4 hours C. 6 hours D. 30 minutes
2. What is the minimum internal cooking temperature for ground chicken? A. 135°F for 15 seconds B. 155°F for 15 seconds C. 165°F for 15 seconds D. 145°F for 15 seconds
3. You just thawed food in the microwave, what should you do next? A. Put it in the hot holding equipment B. Cook it using conventional cooking equipment C. Freeze it D. Cool it down to 41°F

Notes:

CH 7 Service

Holding Food for Service

Any food that is being held for service is at risk and policies must be in place in order to control this risk. The major guidelines are as follows:

- Food covers and sneeze guards must be used
- Hold foods at the correct temperature
  HOT - 135°F or higher and COLD - 41°F or lower
- Check the foods internal temperature regularly and at least every 4 hours. Discard food that is not the correct temperature.
- Never use hot holding equipment to reheat food

Holding Food Without Temperature Control (TPHC)
You may need to hold food without temperature control i.e a catered event. If so there are certain conditions that must be met.

For Cold Food
Cold food can be held for up to 6 hours without temperature control IF:

- The food was 41°F or below before it was removed from refrigeration
- The food was labeled with the time it was removed and the time it needs to be thrown out
- The food must not exceed 70°F while it is being served.
- Sell, serve or discard food after 6 hours.

For Hot Food
Hot food can be held for up to 4 hours without temperature control IF:

- The food was 135°F before it was removed from temperature control
- The food was labeled with the time it was removed and the time it needs to be thrown out
- Sell, serve or discard food after 4 hours.

Serving Food

Contamination is one of the number one risk factors during the service of food. You can train your staff to prevent contamination by doing the following:

- *Single Use Gloves* must be used when handling ready to eat foods. There are some situations where bare hand contact is allowed. This was previously discussed.
- *Clean and Sanitize all utensils* before use and use separate utensils for each task.

- *Serving utensils* need to be stored above the rim of the food.
- *When refilling take-home containers* make sure they were provided by the establishment for this purpose and that they are clean and sanitized.
- Staff must hold plate ware and utensils by surfaces that will not come into *contact with the guests' mouth*.
- Silverware that has been preset ***cannot be re-used*** unless it was wrapped in a rollup napkin.

Never re-serve food from one guest to another, unless the food was pre-packaged and sealed as to prevent contamination. i.e. coffee creamers, ketchup packets or chips in a bag.

Self service areas must protect the food from contamination from the guest by using a sneeze guard or by using a display case. Wrapping the food in plastic wrap or coverings is also acceptable.

Chapter 7 QUICK QUIZ *(answers on page 41)*
1. At what temperature must hot food be held? A. 135°F B. 145°F C. 165° D. 155°
2. Which of the following temperatures is safe for cooking raw ground chicken? (circle one) A. 39° B. 125°F C. 165°F D. 69°
3. How often must the temperature of raw steak be checked while being held cold? (circle one) A. 41° or below B. every 4 hours C. every 2 hours D. every 6 hours

Notes:

CH 8 Food Safety Management Systems

In order to ensure you are serving safe food you will want to provide written food safety **practices and procedures** on all of the following for your employees.

Personal hygiene
Training systems
Suppliers
Cleaning and sanitizing
Standard operating procedures (SOP's)
Facility and equipment maintenance
Pest control

These procedures can be enforced through a system called ***Active Managerial Control.*** Active managerial control critical to the success of an operation. The Manager or PIC should:

- *Monitoring* critical activities in the operation
- Taking the necessary ***corrective action*** when required
- *Verify* that the actions are taking control of the risks factors

HACCP- Hazard Analysis and Critical Control Points
HACCP is difficult to understand but it is an extremely detailed food safety management program that relies on not missing any details within your process that may cause someone to become sick or injured. HACCP is written to address a specific process or recipe, imagine you are trying to write out instruction for a 6 year old to safely cook a burger from beginning to end.

There are 7 HACCP principles that need to be addressed.

1. Conduct a hazard analysis
2. Determine critical control points
3. Set critical limits
4. Develop monitoring procedures
5. Set up corrective actions
6. Verification
7. Record keeping and documentation

- *Conduct a Hazard Analysis* – Look at all the ingredients used and decide which will be at risk and what risks for each of those ingredients are.
- **Example** – The burger patty is made with ground
- beef and the hazard is E-coli.

- *Determining Critical Control Points (CCPs)* – The critical control points are points in time during the flow of food where the foodborne hazard can be prevented, reduced or eliminated.
- *Examples*
  - Receiving the burger patty from the supplier
  - Storing the patty correctly until preparation preventing cross contamination
  - Cooking the burger patty reduces the risk of E-coli.

- *Establish Critical Limits* – Identify the actual temperature or limit that prevents the hazard.
- *Example* – During cooking burger patties the critical limit is a minimum internal cooking temp of 155°F.

- *Establishing Monitoring Procedures* – How will the food be monitored and by whom and how often to ensure the critical limit has been met.
- *Example* – A food handler monitors the cooking process of the burger patty to ensure it has been properly cooked.

- *Identifying corrective actions* - Determine what may go wrong and what action needs to be taken when an unanticipated hazard or critical control limit isn't met.
- *Example* – A food handler checking the temperature of a burger patty and reading it at 143°F degrees then returning it back to the grill to continue cooking to 155°F.

- *Verify that the system works* – Review the records that were kept throughout the flow of food to ensure all limits were met and procedures were followed.
- *Example* - At the end of the day, a manager looking over all recording done by food handlers at all points of the cooking process for hamburger patties.

- *Establish Procedures for Record Keeping and Documentation* – Maintaining the HACCP plan and keeping all documentation that were created.
- *Example* – A manager keeps records for the burger patty HACCP plan for 2 years after the burger has been cooked.

Chapter 8 QUICK QUIZ *(answers on page 41)*
1. When a food manager finds a problem how do they fix it? (circle one) A. monitoring B. critical control points C. record keeping D. corrective action
2. What procedure would require a HACCP plan? (circle one) A. serving rare steak B. holding chicken without temperature control C. FDA D. sous vide
3. What is the second step of a HACCP plan? (circle one) A. Receiving B. Hazard Analysis C. Washing D. critical control points

Notes:

CH 9 Facilities and Pest Prevention

You must choose the equipment that you use in your facility carefully because they will need to be able withstand repeated cleaning.

Use materials that are ***non-porous*** such as stainless steel and FRP. Also, any place that the floor meets the wall will be hard to clean so you are required to place a curved edge here called ***coving or base cove***.

And all equipment must meet NSF standards for durability, cleanability and resistance to damage.

All floor mounted equipment must be on movable casters (wheels) or ***6 inches*** off of the ground for cleaning purposes. It can also be sealed to the ground.

Counter top equipment must be ***4 inches*** above the counter, movable or sealed.

Handwashing stations must be conveniently located and are required in:

- Restrooms or directly next to them
- Food-prep areas
- Service areas
- Dishwashing areas

Make sure they are accessible and that employees are only using them for handwashing.

Handwashing stations must be equipped with all of the following:

- Hot and cold running water
- Soap
- Paper towels or a warm air dryer
- Signage
- Garbage container

Cross-connection:
Physical link between safe water and dirty water from

- Drains
- Sewers
- Other wastewater sources

Back Flow: Reverse flow of contaminants through a cross connection to the drinkable

water supply.
Back Siphonage: A vacuum created by the plumbing system that sucks contaminants into the water supply.

A ***vacuum breaker*** is a mechanical device that prevents backsiphonage. It does this by closing a check valve and sealing the water supply line shut when water flow is stopped.

An ***air gap*** is an air space that separates a water supply outlet from a potentially contaminated source. We see them in floor drains and tall faucets above the flood rim of the sink.

Lighting

Consider the following when installing and maintaining lighting: Different areas of the facility have different lighting intensity requirements. Local jurisdictions usually require prep areas to be brighter than other areas. All lights should have shatter-resistant lightbulbs or protective covers. Replace burned out bulbs with correct size bulbs.
Ventilation systems:

- Must be cleaned and maintained to prevent grease and condensation from building up on walls and ceilings
- Follow manufacturer's recommendations
- Meet local regulatory requirements

Garbage

Garbage can attract pests and contaminate food, equipment, and utensils if not handled correctly. Staff must be careful when removing garbage so they do not contaminate food or food-contact surfaces.

Clean the inside and outside of garbage containers frequently. This will help prevent the contamination of food and food-contact surfaces. It will also reduce odors and pests. Do not clean garbage containers near prep or food- storage areas.
Indoor containers must be:

- Leak proof, waterproof, and pest proof
- Easy to clean
- Covered when not in use

Designated storage areas:

- Store waste and recyclables separately from food and food-contact surfaces
- Storage must not create a nuisance or a public health hazard

Outdoor containers must:

- Be placed on a smooth, durable, nonabsorbent surface

- Asphalt or concrete
- Have tight-fitting lids
- Be covered at all times
- Have their drain plugs in place

Imminent health hazard: A significant threat or danger to health. Requires immediate correction or closure to prevent injury.

- Electrical power outage
- Fire
- Flood
- Sewage back up

Pest Prevention

Three rules of pest prevention:

- Prevent access to the building
- Check deliveries before they enter the operation by refusing shipments if pests or signs of pests (egg cases, body parts, feces) are found
- Make sure all of the points where pests can access the building are secure by screening windows and vents, sealing cracks in floors and walls, and around pipes and installing air curtains (also called air doors or fly fans) above or alongside doors
- Deny access to food, water, and shelter
- Keep the place clean and constantly be rotating products and equipment to ensure pests don't have a place to hide
- Pest Control Operator (PCO)
- Even after you have made every effort to keep pests out, they may still get into your operation. Work with a PCO to get them under control. Even if you only spot a few pests, they may actually be present in large numbers. Infestations can be very difficult to eliminate. Look for feces, nests, and damage on products, packaging, and the facility itself. Contact your PCO immediately.

Your PCO may ask you for the signs of specific pests such as cockroaches and rodents. Rodents chew on things to grind their teeth down, their teeth never stop growing. You may also find they leave small dark pellets as feces and build nests for their young. Roaches smell terrible, like rancid oil, and their feces looks like pepper. Also, look out for castings and egg shells.

***Chapter 9 QUICK QUIZ** (answers on page 41)*

1. How far off of the ground must equipment be mounted? (circle one) A. 18 inches B. 10 inches C. 6 inches D. 4 inches
2. Which of the following is required in a handwashing station? (circle one) A. Hand Sanitizer B. Soap C. eyewash D. nail brush

3 Which of the following is the sign of a cockroach infestation ? (circle one) A. Nests B. dark pellets C. oily odor D. gnaw marks

Notes:

CH 10 Cleaning and Sanitizing

Cleaning: The process of removing food or dirt from any surface. All things in a food service operation must be cleaned from the floors and the walls to the plates and the counters. For this we will use detergents and scrubbers.

Sanitizing: The process reducing pathogens from an already cleaned food contact to a safe enough level to be used for food. Items must first be cleaned before they can be sanitized. Surfaces can be sanitized by using heat or chemicals.

Heat Sanitizing- Items must be immersed in 171° water for 30 seconds

Chemical Sanitizing

- Chlorine (bleach)
- Iodine
- Quaternary ammonia sanitizer (quat)

In order for chemical sanitizing to be effective five factors must be in place. Most important are concentration and contact time.

- *Concentration*- You must test the chemical solutions in you facility regularly with a test kit and when it appears dirty or may have lost its concentration
- *Contact time*- Each sanitizer differs in the amount of time required for it to be effective
- *Temperature*- Most chemicals require the solution to be cool or cold. Generally room temperature is fine
- *Water Hardness*- Check manufacturers recommendations
- *Water ph*- Check manufacturers recomendations

	Chlorine	Iodine	Quat
Concentration	50-99 ppm	12.5-25 ppm	Follow manufacturers guidelines
Contact Time	≥7 seconds	≥30	≥30

How to clean and sanitize

1. *Scrape or remove food bits from the surface*. Use the correct cleaning tool such as a nylon brush or pad, or a cloth towel.
2. *Wash the surface*. Prepare the cleaning solution with an approved detergent. Wash the surface with the correct cleaning tool such as a cloth towel.
3. *Rinse the surface* with clean water or the correct tool such as a spryer or a clean cloth towel.
4. *Sanitize the surface*. Use the correct sanitizing solution. Prepare the

concentration per manufacturer requirements. Use the correct tool, such as a cloth towel, to sanitize the surface. Make sure the entire surface has come in contact with the sanitizing solution.

5. *Allow the surface to air-dry* to prevent re-contaminating with the towel.

It is also important to when to clean and sanitize. Food-contact surfaces must be cleaned and sanitized:

- After they are used
- Before working with a different type of food
- Any time a task was interrupted and the items may have been contaminated
- After four hours if the items are in constant use

Cleaning and sanitizing stationary equipment:

1. Unplug the equipment
2. Take the removable parts off the equipment
3. Wash, rinse, and sanitize them by hand or run the parts through a dishwasher if allowed
4. Scrape or remove food from the equipment surfaces
5. Wash the equipment surfaces
6. Rinse the equipment surfaces with clean water
7. Sanitize the equipment surfaces
8. Make sure the sanitizer comes in contact with each surface
9. Allow all surfaces to air-dry
10. Put the unit back together

Dishwashing machines

Guidelines:

- Clean the machine as often as needed
- Scrape, rinse, or soak items before washing
- Use the correct dish racks
- NEVER overload dish racks
- Air-dry all items
- Check the machine's water temperature and pressure

High-temperature machines:

- Final sanitizing rinse must be at least 180°F (82°C)
- Temperature of sanitized surfaces must be measured by using either temperature sensitive tape or a maximum registering thermometer

Chemical sanitizing machines clean and sanitize at much lower temperatures. Follow the temperature guidelines provided by the manufacturer.

Manual Dishwashing

Setting up a three-compartment sink:

- Clean and sanitize each sink and drain board

- Fill the first sink with detergent and water at least 110°F (43°C)
- Fill the second sink with clean rinse water
- Fill the third sink with water and sanitizer to the correct concentration
- Provide a clock with a second hand to let food handlers know how long items have been in the sanitizer

When storing clean and sanitized tableware and equipment:

- Store them at least six inches (15 cm) off the floor
- Clean and sanitize drawers and shelves before items are stored
- Store glasses and cups upside down on a clean and sanitized shelf or rack
- Store flatware and utensils with handles up
- Cover the food-contact surfaces of stationary equipment until ready to use
- Clean and sanitize trays and carts used to carry clean tableware and utensils

Cleaning up after people who get sick:

Diarrhea and vomit in the operation must be cleaned up correctly

It can carry Norovirus, which is highly contagious

Correct cleanup can prevent food from becoming contaminated and keep others from getting sick

Consider the following when developing a plan for cleaning up vomit and diarrhea:

- How you will contain liquid and airborne substances, and remove them from the operation
- How you will clean, sanitize, and disinfect surfaces
- When to throw away food that may have been contaminated
- What equipment is needed to clean up these substances, and how it will be cleaned and disinfected after use
- When a food handler must wear personal protective equipment
- How staff will be notified of the correct procedures for containing, cleaning, and disinfecting these substances
- How to segregate contaminated areas from other areas
- When staff must be restricted from working with or around food or excluded from working in the operation
- How sick customers will be quickly removed from the operation
- How the cleaning plan will be implemented

Store cleaning tools and chemicals in a separate area away from food and prep areas

The storage area should have:

- Good lighting so chemicals can be easily seen
- service sink for filling buckets and washing cleaning tools
- Floor drain for dumping dirty water
- Hooks for hanging cleaning tools

NEVER:

- Dump mop water or other liquid waste into toilets or urinals
- Clean tools in sinks used for
- Handwashing
- Food prep
- Dishwashing

Chemicals:

- Only purchase those approved for use in foodservice operations (i.e. no engine degreaser)
- Store them in their original containers away from food and food prep areas
- If transferring it into a new container label the new container with the common name of the chemical

Chemical documentation:

- Keep SDS's for each chemical [instructions for using chemicals]
- When throwing chemicals out
    - Follow local regulatory requirements
    - Must be accessible to employees
    - Follow instructions on the label

To develop an effective cleaning program:

- Create a master cleaning schedule
- Train your staff to follow it
- Monitor the program to make sure it works

Chapter 10 QUICK QUIZ (answers on page 41)

1. What must the temperature of the water be when using the heat sanitizing method? (circle one) A. 171° B. 165°F C. 100° D. 110°

2. Which of the following chemicals is safe for sanitizing in a food service operation? (circle one) A. vinegar B. ammonia C. degreaser D. lemon

3. What is the 4th step of cleaning and sanitizing? (circle one) A. rinse B. sanitize C. air dry D. scrape

Quick Quiz Answers Ch1 1.A 2.C 3.B CH2 1.A 2.A 3.D CH3 1.B 2.C 3.B CH4 1.A 2.C 3.B CH5 1.B 2.C 3.D CH6 1.A 2.C 3.B CH7 1.A 2.C 3.B CH8 1.D 2.D 3.D CH9 1.C 2.B 3.C CH10 1.A 2.B 3.B

Notes:

Practice Test Questions

Circle the best answer to each question below. Be sure to answer all 80 questions.

1 The purpose of a food safety management system is to
A keep all areas of the facility clean and pest-free.
B identify, tag, and repair faulty equipment within the facility.
C prevent foodborne illness by controlling risks and hazards.
D use the correct methods for purchasing and receiving food.

2 A manager's responsibility to actively control risk factors for foodborne illnesses is called
A hazard analysis critical control point (HACCP).
B quality control and assurance.
C food safety management.
D active managerial control.

3 A manager asks a chef to continue cooking chicken breasts after seeing them cooked to an incorrect temperature.
This is an example of which step in active managerial control?
A Identifying risks
B Monitoring
C Corrective action
D Re-evaluation

4 A manager walks around the kitchen every hour to answer questions and to see if staff members are following procedures.
This is an example of which step in active managerial control?
A Management oversight
B Corrective action
C Re-evaluation
D Identify risks

5 One way for managers to show that they know how to keep food safe is to
A become certified in food safety.
B take cooking temperatures.
C monitor employee behaviors.
D conduct self-inspections.

6 A power outage has left hot TCS food out of temperature control for six hours. What must be done with the food?
A Cool the food to 41°F (5°C) or lower.
B Serve the food immediately.
C Cook the food 165°F (74°C).
D Throw the food away.

7 An imminent health hazard, such as a water supply interruption, requires immediate correction or
A a HACCP plan.
B closure of the operation.
C evaluation of the situation.
D normal operating procedures.

8 What is the best way to protect food from deliberate tampering?
A Make it as difficult as possible for someone to tamper with it.
B Allow former employees into the operation.
C Perform spot inspections on new vendors.
D Use the USDA A.L.A.R.M. system.

9 To prevent the deliberate contamination of food, a manager should know whom to contact about suspicious activity,
monitor the security of products, keep information related to food security on file, and know

A when to register with the EPA.
B how to fill out an incident report.
C where to find Safety Data Sheets in the operation.
D who is in the facility.

10 Where should food handlers wash their hands?

A Prep sink
B Utility sink
C Designated sink for handwashing
D Three-compartment sink

11 What must food handlers do after touching their body or clothing?

A Wash their hands
B Rinse their gloves
C Change their aprons
D Use a hand antiseptic

12 When washing hands, what is the minimum time that food handlers should scrub hands and arms with soap?

A 5 seconds
B 8 seconds
C 10 seconds
D 18 seconds

13 After which activity must food handlers wash their hands?

A Clearing tables
B Putting on gloves
C Serving customers
D Applying hand antiseptic

14 What is the main reason for food handlers to avoid scratching their scalps?

A Transferring a food allergen
B Spreading pathogens to the food
C Getting food in their hair
D Causing toxic-metal poisoning

15 When may food handlers wear plain-band rings?

A At any time
B When not handling food
C Only if wearing gloves
D Only if washing dishes

16 What should a food handler do when working with an infected cut on the finger?

A Cover the wound with a bandage.
B Stay away from food and prep areas.
C Cover the hand with a glove or a finger cot.
D Cover the wound with an impermeable bandage or finger cot and a glove.

17 What is the only jewelry that may be worn on the hands or arms while handling food?

A Plain-band ring
B Medical ID bracelet
C Leather-band watch
D Diamond ring

18 In addition to other criteria, how many people must have the same symptoms in order for a foodborne illness to be
considered an outbreak?

A At least 1
B At least 2
C At least 10
D At least 20

19 When should a food handler with a sore throat and fever be excluded from the operation?

A Customers served are primarily a high-risk population

B Fever is over 100°F (38°C)

C Sore throat has lasted for more than 5 days

D Before the regulatory authority is notified

20What is a basic characteristic of a virus?

A Destroyed by cooking

B Grows in food

C Requires a living host to grow

D Commonly found in cattle intestines

21 After handling raw meat and before handling produce, what should food handlers do with their gloves?

A Clean and sanitize them.

B Continue working with them.

C Set them aside if working with meat again later.

D Wash hands and change them.

22 Where should personal items, like a coat, be stored in the operation?

A On a shelf, above food

B On a shelf, below food

C In a designated area, away from food

D In a kitchen, away from moving equipment

23 What should food handlers do after prepping food and before using the restroom?

A Wash their hands

B Take off their hats

C Change their gloves

D Take off their aprons

24 How should the temperature of a shipment of sour cream be taken when it arrives at an operation?

A Place a hand on a container to see if it is cool to the touch.

B Hold an infrared thermometer as close as possible to a case.

C Place the thermometer stem between shipping boxes for a reading.

D Remove the lid of a container and put the thermometer stem into the sour cream.

25 Ice crystals on a frozen food item indicate

A time-temperature abuse.

B cross-contamination.

C poor cleaning and sanitizing.

D poor personal hygiene.

26 What is the most important factor in choosing an approved food supplier?

A It has a HACCP program or other food safety system.

B It has documented manufacturing and packing practices.

C Its warehouse is close to the operation, reducing shipping time.

D It has been inspected and complies with local, state, and federal laws.

27 Which item should be rejected?

A Bags of organic cookies in torn packaging

B Bottled milk at 41°F (5°C)

C Single-use cups in original packing

D Live oysters with an internal temperature of 50°F (10°C)

28 Supplies should be stored away from the walls and at least off of the floor.
A 2 inches (5 centimeters)
B 4 inches (10 centimeters)
C 5 inches (13 centimeters)
D 6 inches (15 centimeters)

29 Soup on a buffet should be labeled with the
A name of the food.
B prep date.
C soup's ingredients.
D use-by date.

30 How should chemicals be stored?
A Above food
B Away from prep areas
C In food storage areas
D With kitchenware

31 What should be done to ready-to-eat TCS food that will be prepped on-site and held for longer than 24 hours?
A Date mark it.
B Sell it.
C Throw it away.
D Serve it within the next hour.

32 What must a manager do with a recalled food item in the operation?
A Combine the item with non-recalled items during preparation.
B Record the names of customers who purchase the item.
C Store the recalled item separately from other food.
D Sell all recalled items within 24 hours.

33 A recall has been issued for a specific brand of orange juice. The store manager has matched the information from the recall notice to the item, removed the item from inventory, and stored it in a secure location. What should the manager do next?
A Refer to the vendor notification for next steps.
B Contact the supplier and arrange for the product to be picked up.
C Label the item to prevent it from accidently being placed back in inventory.
D Inform the local media, customers, and employees of the reason for the recall.

34 A food item that is received with an expired use-by date should be
A rejected.
B used immediately.
C accepted but labeled differently.
D accepted but kept separate from other items

35 Cold food can be held intentionally without temperature control for hours as long as it does not exceed 70°F (21°C).
A 2
B 4
C 6
D 8

36 When delivering food for off-site service, raw poultry must be stored
A at a lower temperature than ready-to-eat food.
B separately from ready-to-eat food.
C without temperature control.
D above raw beef.

37 What is the minimum internal cooking temperature for seafood?
A 135°F (57°C) or higher for 15 seconds
B 145°F (63°C) or higher for 15 seconds
C 155°F (68°C) or higher for 15 seconds
D 165°F (74°C) or higher for 15 seconds

38 Food must be cooled from 135°F (57°C) to within 2 hours.
A 80°F (27°C)
B 45°F (7°C)
C 70°F (21°C)
D 41°F (5°C)

39 Hot TCS food being hot-held for service must be at what temperature?
A 70°F (21°C) or above
B 125°F (52°C) or above
C 135°F (57°C) or above
D 155°F (68°C) or above

40 Which method is a safe way to thaw food?
A As part of the cooking process
B Under running water at 125°F (52°C) or higher
C Submerged in a sink of standing water at 70°F (21°C)
D On the counter at room temperature

41 Food being cooled must pass quickly through which temperature range to reduce pathogen growth?
A 65°F to 20°F (18°C to -6°C)
B 125°F to 70°F (52°C to 21°C)
C 180°F to 130°F (82°C to 54°C)
D 220°F to 195°F (104°C to 90°C)

42 What food item does the FDA advise against offering on a children's menu?
A Rare cheeseburgers
B Cheese pizza
C Peanut butter and jelly sandwiches
D Fried shrimp

43 A food handler with a sore throat and a fever should be excluded from working in a day-care center, because the children
A will not receive the same level of service.
B could make the food handler more sick.
C are a high-risk population.
D will refuse to eat.

44 Which is a chemical contaminant?
A Bones in a chicken fillet
B Norovirus in shellfish
C Metal shavings in a can of peaches
D Tomato juice served in a pewter pitcher

45 Which is a biological contaminant?
A Bones in a chicken fillet
B Norovirus in shellfish
C Metal shavings in a can of peaches
D Tomato juice served in a pewter pitcher

46 The 6 conditions bacteria need to grow are food, acidity, temperature, time, oxygen, and
A meat.
B moisture.
C melatonin.
D management.

47 Using the same knife to chop carrots for a salad immediately after cutting up raw chicken is an example of
A time-temperature abuse.
B cross-contamination.
C poor personal hygiene.
D purchasing from an unapproved supplier.

48 Which is an example of physical contamination?
A Sneezing on food
B Touching dirty food-contact surfaces
C Bones in fish
D Cooking tomato sauce in a copper pan

49 Which symptom could mean a customer is having an allergic reaction to food?

A Coughing

B Dehydration

C Swollen lips

D Sneezing

50 To prevent food allergens from being transferred to food,

A clean and sanitize utensils before preparing an allergen special order.

B buy food from trusted suppliers.

C store cold food at 41°F (5°C) or lower.

D avoid pewter tableware and utensils and copper cookware.

51 Which is a Big Eight food allergen?

A Broccoli

B Wheat

C Grapes

D Pork

52 What is the minimum temperature that must be maintained when holding hot soup for service?

A 100°F (38°C)

B 120°F (49°C)

C 135°F (57°C)

D 155°F (68°C)

53 Cold food being held without temperature control for up to six hours cannot exceed which temperature while it is being served?

A 41°F (5°C)

B 50°F (10°C)

C 60°F (16°C)

D 70°F (21°C)

54 A food handler has been holding chicken salad for sandwiches in a cold well for seven hours.

When she checks the temperature of the chicken salad, it is 54°F (12°C). What must the food handler do?

A Sell the remaining chicken salad immediately

B Sell the remaining chicken salad within 2 hours

C Cool the chicken salad to 41°F (5°C)

D Discard the chicken salad

Practice Tests and Answer Keys Diagnostic Test

55 A food handler working in a hotel removes cold tuna salad from the cooler at 9:00 am and delivers it to a conference for an 11:00 am buffet luncheon, where it is held without temperature control. By what time must the tuna salad be served or thrown out?

A 12:00 p.m.

B 2:00 p.m.

C 3:00 p.m.

D 4:00 p.m.

56 An operation has a buffet with 8 different items on it. How many serving utensils are needed to serve the items on the buffet?

A 1

B 2

C 4

D 8

57 Which food item may be handled with bare hands?

A Sliced cheese for sandwiches

B Boiled egg slices for salad

C Chopped carrots for stew

D Parsley for garnish

58 A cook wore single-use gloves while forming raw ground beef into patties. The cook continued to wear them while slicing hamburger buns. What mistake was made?

A The cook did not wear reusable gloves while handling the raw ground beef and hamburger buns.

B The cook did not clean and sanitize the gloves before handling the hamburger buns.

C The cook did not wash hands before putting on the same gloves to slice the hamburger buns.

D The cook did not wash hands and put on new gloves before slicing the hamburger buns.

59 When must a consumer advisory be provided for menu items containing TCS food?

A When the item is raw or undercooked.

B When the item contains a potential allergen.

C When the operation provides only counter service.

D When the operation primarily serves a high-risk population.

60 Which feature is most important for a chemical storage area?

A Good lighting

B Single-use towels

C Nonskid floor mats

D Emergency shower system

61 What is the correct way to store mops in between uses?

A Propped in a corner

B In a clean bucket

C In a utility sink

D Hanging on a hook

62 A buser poured some cleaner from its original container into a smaller working container. What else does the buser need to do?

A Label the working container with its contents.

B Read the safety data sheet (SDS) for the cleaner.

C Use a new wiping cloth when first using the working container.

D Note on the original container that some cleaner was put into a working container.

63 Which does not require sanitizing?

A Plates

B Knives

C Walls

D Tongs

64 Which surfaces must be both cleaned and sanitized?

A Walls

B Cutting boards

C Storage shelves

D Garbage containers

65 The first step in cleaning and sanitizing items in a three-compartment sink is

A air-drying items.

B washing items in detergent.

C immersing items in sanitizer.

D rinsing, scraping, or soaking items.

66 After scraping and washing, what is the third step in cleaning and sanitizing a prep table?

A Sanitizing

B Air-drying

C Rinsing

D Rewashing

67 In a heat-sanitizing dishwasher, what is the minimum temperature for the final rinse?

A 152°F (67°C)

B 180°F (82°C)

C 192°F (89°C)

D 200°F (93°C)

68 A food-contact surface must be cleaned and sanitized

A before working with a different type of food.

B every 6 hours.

C only if the food handler changes gloves.

D at the end of the food handler's shift.

69 Where should garbage cans be cleaned?

A Away from food and utensils

B Next to food-prep areas

C In dishwashing areas

D In food storage areas

70 When the kitchen garbage can was full, an employee placed the full garbage bag on a prep table and tied it securely. Then he carried it to the Dumpster and disposed of it. What was done incorrectly?

A The employee waited until the garbage was full.

B The bag was disposed of in a dumpster.

C The bag was placed on a prep table.

D The employee tied the bag shut.

71 Grease and condensation buildup on surfaces can be avoided with correct

A garbage disposal.

B lighting.

C sanitizing.

D ventilation.

72 To prevent backflow, a sink must be equipped with a(n)

A Air gap

B Vacuum assist

C Overflow drain

D Touchless controls

73 What are the most important food safety features to look for when selecting flooring, wall, and ceiling materials?

A Absorbent and durable

B Hard and durable

C Porous and durable

D Smooth and durable

74 What information should a master cleaning schedule contain?

A What should be cleaned and when

B What should be cleaned, when, and by whom

C What should be cleaned, when, by whom, and how

D What should be cleaned, when, by whom, how, and why

75 A handwashing station should have hot and cold water, soap, a way to dry hands, and a

A garbage container.

B second timer.

C clock.

D gloves.

76 A food handler drops the end of a hose into a mop bucket and turns the water on to fill it.

What has the food handler done wrong?

A Created a cross-connection

B Created an air-gap separation

C Prevented backflow

D Prevented atmospheric vacuuming

77 The water provided to a handwashing sink must be

A hot water only.

B cold water only.

C potable water only.

D fluoridated water only.

78 Which individual should apply pesticides in a foodservice operation?

A A pest control operator

B A shift manager

C A busboy

D A cook

79 A food handler who is receiving a food delivery observes signs of pests in the food. What should be done?

A The head chef should be warned of the pests.

B The food handler should remove all evidence of the pests.

C The shipment should be refused and prevented from entering the operation.

D The shipment should be stored outside the kitchen until a manager inspects it.

80 How high must legs be on table-mounted equipment?

A At least 1 inch (3 centimeters)

B At least 2 inches (5 centimeters)

C At least 4 inches (10 centimeters)

D At least 6 inches (15 centimeters)

ANSWERS

1 c
2 d
3 c
4 a
5 a
6 d
7 b
8 a
9 d
10 c
11 a
12 c
13 a
14 b
15 a
16 d
17 a
18 b
19 a
20 c
21 d
22 c
23 d
24 d
25 s
26 d
27 a
28 d
29 a
30 b
31 a
32 c
33 c
34 a

35 v
36 b
37 b
38 c
39 c
40 a
41 b
42 a
43 c
44 d
45 b
46 b
47 b
48 c
49 c
50 a
51 b
52 c
53 d
54 d
55 c
56 d
57 c
58 d
59 a
60 a
61 d
62 a
63 c
64 b
65 d
66 c
67 b
68 a
69 a
70 c
71 d
72 a
73 d
74 c
75 a
76 a
77 c
78 a
79 c
80 c

Made in the USA
Middletown, DE
16 October 2023